AN EASY GUIDE TO MEDITATION

ROY EUGENE DAVIS

I salute the supreme teacher,
the Truth, whose Nature is Bliss;
who is the giver of the highest
happiness; who is pure wisdom;
who is beyond all qualities and
infinite like the sky; who is beyond
words; who is one and eternal,
pure and still; who is beyond all
change and phenomena and who
is the silent witness to all our
thoughts and emotions—I salute
Truth, the supreme teacher.
— *Ancient Vedic Hymn*

CSA PRESS, PUBLISHERS
CENTER FOR SPIRITUAL AWARENESS
Lakemont, Georgia 30552

978-0-87707-244-7

CSA Press
PO Box 7 Lakemont, Georgia 30552-0001

Telephone 706-782-4723   Fax 706-782-4560
csainc@csa-davis.org   www.csa-davis.org

The publishing department of
Center for Spiritual Awareness

Printed in the United States of America

Contents

Introduction

The period in human history through which we are now passing is characterized by rapid changes in the outer realm, while indications of accelerated intellectual growth and spiritual awakening are increasingly observable in the transformations occurring in the social order. That we are being confronted by effects of powerful evolutionary causes is obvious to anyone who is sufficiently perceptive to examine the evidence. I look upon the world scene with an abiding sense of wonder and am serenely optimistic about our near and distant future possibilities. I hope you are viewing the unfolding drama of life with a thankful heart and pronouncing it good.

Because of these unfolding circumstances, and the widespread interest in matters related to facilitating expanded states of consciousness and improving functional abilities, the information in this edition of *An Easy Guide to Meditation* will, I feel, be helpful to many readers. The first book issued under this title was published in 1978 and distributed in many editions in several countries. Now, to make the message even more widely available, the text has been newly written, the format is designed for convenient reference, and the price is within the means of anyone with a sincere interest in the subject.

After reading this book, and putting into practice

some of the recommended routines, please consider sharing copies with people whom you know to be interested in enhancing their lives. Having a harmonious relationship with the Presence and Power that produced the realm of nature and enlivens it, and which, ultimately, determines satisfying outcomes for all worthwhile endeavors, is certainly a most favorable condition for all of us.

During my early teenage years I pondered the meaning of life and aspired to clearly know it. Near the end of my eighteenth year I was fortunate to meet my guru Paramahansa Yogananda in Los Angeles, California, and to be accepted by him for training. Now, as I write these words, forty-five years have passed; each has provided invaluable opportunities for continued spiritual growth and service. I have traveled the world to share this information and have discovered that, behind the screens of social fabric and cultural influences, all people are, at the core, the same: that one, divine essence is the reality of us all.

Everything I recommend in these pages, I do, or have done. The basic principles, practices, and guidelines are universal. I did not originate them. They are not mine, nor do they belong to anyone. Some of the insights shared here, and explanations of how I view our relationship with the Infinite, are my own because I, like everyone else, see from my personal perspective. Take to heart whatever is meaningful to you. Use your intellectual skills to determine the meaning of whatever is not immediately clear to you.

Use your intuitive abilities to see beyond words and concepts, to truth—that which is factual. Doing this is the only approach to understanding the processes of life that will satisfy your heart.

If you are a beginning meditator, the guidelines in the early chapters will be sufficient to enable you to practice with benefit. If you a more experienced meditator, review your practice to be sure you are doing it correctly, then use the various techniques and procedures to improve your meditative skills. Even if you are not inspired when you first sit to meditate, sit still anyway, and wait in the silence. In time, your innate, soul urge to have awareness restored to flawless clarity will implement the meditation process and direct its actions to a successful conclusion.

Planet Earth is our present dwelling place but it is not our permanent abode. Where did we come from? Why are we here? What are we supposed to do while here? What will become of us when we depart this world? How can we awaken to higher understanding and live with meaningful purpose? These are questions we should ask until the true answers are known. I pray that the allness of life becomes known to you, and that all your needs are met and your destiny is fulfilled.

Roy Eugene Davis

Lakemont, Georgia

CHAPTER ONE

Meditation as a Foundation Practice for Personal Benefits and Authentic Spiritual Growth

Meditation, correctly practiced, is the simple process of removing attention from conditions and circumstances which, when cognized and overly identified with, fragment and cloud our perceptions. Meditating, while remaining alert and observant, enables us to easily experience pure (clear) levels of awareness or states of consciousness. Doing this on a regular schedule provides frequent opportunities for physiological and psychological rest, while freeing attention to explore more refined states of consciousness and to effortlessly experience spontaneous unfoldments of innate, spiritual qualities.

Please remember, as you read this book and proceed to the practice of meditation, that the secret of successful meditative experience is to relax into the process, allowing constructive adjustments of mental states and states of consciousness to occur naturally. For this reason, it is recommended that anxiety, as well as any inclination you may have to exert effort to accomplish something, are to be avoided when meditating. Anxiety about the outcome of an endeavor indicates an attitude of need and keeps us too self-centered. A sense of personal effort or excessive use of will power, to accomplish a goal or to make something happen, arises from self-consciousness which needs to be renounced so that more refined levels of awareness can be perceived and experienced.

At all times, whether meditating or routinely engaged in everyday circumstances and relationships, it is helpful to be inwardly aware of the fact that you are an immortal, spiritual being temporarily relating to the human condition. While in this world you express as a Spirit-mind-body being, with your spiritual nature remaining superior to the mind and the physical body.

You need to know that you are a spiritual being so that you can do helpful things to allow your innate qualities to unfold and express. People who are self-consciously identified with their personality characteristics, or with the physical body or objective circumstances, sometimes become forgetful of their essential nature as spiritual beings. Then, if they endeavor to facilitate spiritual growth, they may tend to think in terms of trying to transform their human, conditioned nature into a spiritual one. The truth is, the human condition does not become spiritual; when conditions are ideal, our spiritual nature awakens and blossoms, allowing us to clearly apprehend that we are but using mind and body while the reality of us, our spiritual nature, remains ever what it is. At the innermost core of our being we are individualized (though not independent) units of the omnipresent consciousness of God. Even partial, intellectual understanding of this primary fact of life can enable us to have a more clear, mature perception of ourselves and of our world, and provide us freedom to make rational choices and implement useful actions.

While the primary purpose of meditation practice is to facilitate awakened spiritual consciousness, the side-benefits which contribute to our wellness and improved function are several:

• Mental transformations and thinking processes become more organized as the result of meditative calmness and the influence of refined states of consciousness.

• The body's immune system is strengthened and physiological functions are encouraged to be more balanced and efficient.

• Biologic aging processes are slowed. Older, long-term meditators are mentally and physically younger than their calendar years might suggest.

• Stress symptoms are reduced. The nervous system is refreshed and enlivened, allowing awareness to be more easily processed through it.

• Regenerative energies are awakened. These, directed by innate intelligence, vitalize the body, empower the mind, and have restorative and healing influences.

• Intellectual skills are improved, causing delusions and illusions to be dispelled. Intuition awakens, allowing us to directly know whatever we desire to know and to experience a vivid sense of unerring inner guidance.

- Appreciation for living is enhanced.
- Creativity is stimulated.
- Innate spiritual qualities awaken, enabling us to be more insightful, and functionally skillful.
- Rapid, more satisfying, authentic spiritual growth is nurtured because body, mind, and awareness is beneficially influenced by refined superconscious states.

Spiritual growth is *authentic* when it can be validated by its obvious, beneficial influences and when we can easily demonstrate higher understanding and unrestricted functional abilities. As the defining characteristics and vitality of a living plant can be known by examining the characteristics and quality of fruit it produces, so our states of consciousness and degree of higher understanding can be determined by how we are living our lives and the personal circumstances that prevail. What we do and what we experience has a direct correlation with our habitual states of consciousness and mental states. The more spiritually aware we are, the more harmonious and fulfilling are our lives.

I am not suggesting that we measure spiritual growth by material standards; only that when we are spiritually aware we should spontaneously demonstrate soul-empowered aliveness and enhanced functional abilities. We should have fewer delusions (fixed, erroneous beliefs) and illusions (misperceptions), and be able to function more skillfully. It cannot truthfully be said of us that we are spiritually awake if we continue to exhibit characteristics common to clouded states of awareness, deficiencies in intellectual skills, addictive personality disorders, almost constant frustration of desires, and other kinds of limitation. We may "love God" and feel ourselves to be committed to spiritual growth—and (perhaps) presume ourselves to be quite holy—but if results are not unfolding in constructive, everyday circumstances, we would do well to admit that we have problems that need to be solved and we will not really be fulfilled until they are.

If you are primarily interested in experiencing the life-enhancement benefits of meditation, proceed with dedicated intention; spiritual growth will follow. If you are more focused on spiritual growth, accept the side-benefits as they unfold. Doing so can only make life better and more enjoyable.

Regular meditation is of value to anyone who is able to learn it and adhere to the recommended practice routines. Individuals with disabling mental or emotional problems should not attempt to meditate until they have been restored to a functional degree of wellness. For practice to be effective, the meditator must be able to remain alert and attentive to the process, while being alert and discerning so that distractions are avoided.

If you have a religious affiliation and it is satisfying to you, you need not change it in order to practice meditation. Meditation will enable you to be more soul-centered and God-conscious. With progressive spiritual growth, your understanding of your relationship with the Infinite will improve. You will be more insightful: more intellectually and intuitively capable of discerning the difference between truth and untruth.

Our daily spiritual practice routine, as helpful as it is, represents only a portion of the time we have to live our lives well. How we live every waking moment is just as important as the time and attention we give to our interludes of subjective contemplation. It is in the arena of everyday circumstances and relationships that we are provided ample opportunity to demonstrate what we know and prove to ourselves the depth and clarity of our understanding. If we are not living well—that is, freely and productively— we are not growing spiritually. How we experience life is in direct relationship to our inner condition: to our psychological health and maturity and our understanding of the purpose for living, and what we are willing to do to live our lives successfully.

Therefore, we should not become addicted to our spiritual practice routines or be inclined to indulge ourselves in inner work to the extent that we deny ourselves the privilege (and duty, even) of participating in meaningful activities and relationships. Scheduled sessions of subjective contemplation should be balanced with worthwhile activities. In this way do we fulfill ourselves and the purposes of life itself.

CHAPTER TWO

Experiencing the Natural Process: How to Meditate Effectively

A most useful approach to meditation practice is to consider it the most important activity of each day. Schedule it as you would an extremely important appointment, and unfailingly keep your appointment with the Infinite.

Our lives are meant to be lived effectively and successfully. For this, we need to be alert and functional. Regular, correct practice of meditation can contribute to our overall wellness and enhance our abilities to be knowledgeably and skillfully functional. The most useful result of right meditation practice is that of enabling us to be spiritually aware and conscious of the fact that we are ever anchored in the Infinite Life.

Schedule your practice session at a time when you can give your total attention to the process. Early morning, before starting the day's activities, is an ideal time. If this is not possible, choose a time that is best for you and adhere to it. Some meditators enjoy their practice twice a day: early in the morning after restful sleep, and in late afternoon or early evening. Dedicated practice at least once a day is recommended.

Although not absolutely necessary, it can be helpful to have a private place set aside as your personal meditation sanctuary to be used only for that purpose. Whenever you go there, you will be inclined to avoid thoughts about secular matters and give your attention completely to meditation practice and God-communion.

The routine is easy. Adhere to it without complicating the process and let results unfold naturally. The progressive stages of practice should be clearly understood. They are:

• *Sitting* – The ideal meditation posture is comfortable and pleasant. Sit upright, with attention gently flowing upward to the area between the eyebrows (the spiritual eye center) and the higher brain. This will begin the inward turning process. Be content. Accept the fact that, for the duration of practice, there is nothing more important than what you are presently doing.

• *Beginning* – How you start your practice will be determined by your psychological disposition and your knowledge of the meditation process. You may begin with prayer, to awaken to a sense of attunement with God. However God is real to you, whether as an omnipresent Being, Universal Intelligence, or a Benevolent Presence, pray to God. All soul-impelled prayers go the Source regardless of our concepts or ideas about God. With awakened spiritual consciousness, your understanding of God and your real relationship with God will improve until you actually know and experience God as God really is. Or you may begin with a preferred meditation technique. Proceed however you feel inclined, until you experience physical relaxation and mental calm. At this stage, the body's vital forces are more harmonized and mental and emotional distractions are minimal.

• *Internalization of Attention* – As practice progresses, attention withdraws from externals (from environmental circumstances, and from physical, mental, and emotional conditions). Withdrawn from contact with distracting influences, attention can now be easily directed to the purpose of meditation practice.

• *Concentration* – Perfect concentration is an undisturbed flow of attention to the point of focus.

• *Pure Meditation* – Continuous, uninterrupted flowing of attention to the object being contemplated is pure meditation.

• *The Peak Experience* – When awareness is partially or completely removed from identification with mental processes and transformations, superconsciousness is experienced. Degrees of superconsciousness are determined by whether mental and emotional influences are mixed with superconscious awareness or if restrictions and distractions are absent.

Superconsciousness is natural to the soul. At our innermost level of being, superconsciousness is constant. This is why it can be acknowledged that, at the soul level, everyone is already free. The reason many souls do not know they are free is because

their attention is identified with mental processes
and objective circumstances to the extent that they
have temporarily forgotten their real, inner nature.
Meditation is helpful because it enables us to have
awareness restored to wholeness. When we are not
established in awareness of pure consciousness, we
tend to look outward for a relationship or for support
of some kind. When we are consciously established in
pure consciousness, we are soul-content and always
peaceful. We can then relate to our feelings and
thoughts, and to people and circumstances, more
appropriately.

Everyone experiences a degree of soul content-
ment during deep, dreamless sleep. This is the unconscious way to be open to the restorative influences
of the soul. Meditation practice is the conscious way
to be responsive to enlivening, spiritual influences.
Repeated superconscious episodes eventually purify
the mental field, resulting in mental illumination
and the removal of all delusions and illusions.

A few beginning meditators discover that they can
meditate without having to use a planned procedure
or a specific meditation technique. They simply sit,
turn within, open themselves to the possibility of
experiencing spontaneous adjustments of states of
consciousness, and flow along with the process. However, most beginning meditators do not experience
spontaneous awakenings. Because of habit, their
awareness tends to remain involved with physical
sensations, emotional states, and thought processes.
For them, an intentional approach supported by

knowledgeable practice of a meditation technique, is helpful. Successful use of a time-tested meditation technique—such as prayer, mantra, contemplation of inner light and/or sound—will enable them to remove attention from sources of distraction and bring them to the stage where spontaneous meditation can occur.

Prayer is a direct approach to meditation. One need only pray from the heart (from the soul) for attunement with God and for spiritual awakening. Prayer can continue until it is no longer necessary. Meditation will then spontaneously unfold as impelled by the soul's innate urge to have awareness restored to wholeness.

If you want to use another meditation technique, mantra practice is one of the easiest and most beneficial. The Sanskrit word *mantra* is from *manas* (mind or thinking principle) and *tra* (that which protects and takes beyond). Internal listening to a mantra, a chosen word, word-phrase or a subtle sound, keeps attention focused, thus "protecting" it from being unduly influenced by feelings, moods, or thoughts, "taking it beyond" clouded or confused mental states to clear, superconscious levels. In the following chapter, several mantras are described, along with explanations for their use.

If you are a new meditator, plan to sit for at least 20 minutes, to allow time to experience deep relaxation, settling of emotions and thoughts, and to rest in the tranquil silence. If you are a more experienced meditator, after resting in the silence, proceed to more intentional contemplation. Short meditations of 20 to 30 minutes are ideal for inner refreshment and centering. Longer meditations provide opportunities for more profound exploration of refined states of consciousness and for the unfoldment of spiritual qualities and insightful perceptions. Use this routine on a regular schedule for superior results:

• *Sit to Meditate* – Sit upright, poised and relaxed, with an attitude of alert expectancy. Let your awareness be in the spinal pathway. Withdraw attention from externals, then from the physical senses, turning it upward to the spiritual eye and higher brain.

• *Be Open to the Infinite* – Open your mind and your heart (innermost being, soul) to the Omnipresent Life, to God—as God is known, or as God is mentally pictured by you. Have an attitude of reverence and devotion.

• *Proceed* – If you pray, do so now. If meditation occurs spontaneously, flow with it. If a specific technique (a mantra or any technique you know) will be helpful, use it until you no longer need it, then flow into meditation.

• *Rest in the Peak Experience* – When you awaken to a satisfying level of mental calm, tranquility, and clear awareness, here rest. Remain alert to this experience for as long as it persists. This is the beneficial phase of meditation practice, during which superconscious influences are introduced to the mental field, nervous system, and physiology.

If you are satisfied at this level, when you feel inclined to conclude your practice session, do so. If you want to more intentionally contemplate subtle and refined levels of consciousness or higher realities, do so until you feel inclined to conclude the session.

At the conclusion of your practice session you may remain seated for a few minutes for the purpose of doing some intentional inner work: letting awareness of superconsciousness blend more obviously with mental processes and body awareness, then engaging in possibility-thinking, problem-solving, intercessory prayer, or any other useful activity. Or you may merely return attention to matters at hand and resume your normal relationships and activities.

If pausing after meditation for the purpose of doing intentional inner work, here are some guidelines:

• Rest in the aftereffects tranquility of the meditation experience. Feel that your mind is illumined: radiant with soul light. Know that, from now on, only entirely constructive mental attitudes and thoughts will prevail, and that only entirely worthwhile, constructive impulses will determine desires and actions. Feel yourself to be attuned with Cosmic Mind: that your thoughts and desires are blended with Cosmic Mind and you are responsive to life-enhancing impulses flowing into your mind from Cosmic Mind.

Feel that your body is enlivened by superconscious forces, that illumination extends to, and throughout, your body: strengthening the body's immune system, slowing biologic aging processes, awakening regenerative energies, refining the brain and nervous system, and harmonizing the actions of glands, organs, and systems of the body.

• Feel yourself to be in harmony with the rhythms and flows of the universe. The universe is a series of connected aspects, a continuum. It is self-referring (all of its aspects interact) and self-complete, a wholeness. When you are in accord with its processes, you are included in them and all of your needs are spontaneously provided. You are inspired to right thinking and right action, and events, relationships, and circumstances unfold in entirely supportive ways.

• Acknowledge the innate divinity of every person and wish everyone their highest good, just as you accept your own highest good in all aspects of your life. Wish for all people to be enlightened. Wish for all creatures to be happy and free to fulfill their purposes.

• If you need direction in life, engage in possibility-thinking. Imagine "what can be" and "what you can do" so that your constructive desires can be easily fulfilled and all of your purposes can be actualized or expressed.

• If you are confronting problems, feel confident that every problem has a solution and you can know it. Open your mind to possibilities, see through appearances to desirable outcomes. If a solution does not immediately unfold in your mind and awareness, give the situation to God with absolute faith, then be open to unplanned and uncontrived good fortune. Use your common sense and practical skills to help yourself while knowing that the Power which nurtures the universe, and you, can do anything. There are no unsolvable problems; there are no incurable illnesses; there are no permanent mundane conditions or relationships; and there are no limits to what you, as a spiritual being, can know and accomplish.

• If you need healing of any kind, see through limiting circumstances to conditions which are more ideal, and accept them in your mind and consciousness as being real. Follow through with nurturing actions and behaviors, if necessary. First, be established in the conviction of wholeness and freedom.

• If you want to pray for someone, be inwardly established in awareness of the Presence of God, knowing for yourself that, as God's grace can and will meet your every need, so it can and will meet every need for those with whom you share this interlude of intercessory prayer. Continue in silent, inner work until you feel soul-content and thankful.

Always, when engaged in inner work, first be established in awareness of the Presence of God. The *Presence* of God *is,* as being. The *Power* of God *acts* to make possible expression and effects. When you are established in awareness of the Presence of God, It thinks through your mind, Its inclination is your will, Its impulses impel you to action or inspire you to be still and wait.

The soul, being an individualized unit, ray, or aspect of God's consciousness, has within it all of the characteristics and capacities of God. It would not be accurate to say that we are God, for we are not. What is true is that "God is us." Our role is to consciously know ourselves as we really are, as spiritual beings in relationship to God. When we are fully conscious of what we essentially are, and what our true relationship with God is, we are Self-realized. The word *Self* with an upper case *S* is used in spiritual literature to refer to the soul, the changeless essence, in contrast to an egocentric sense of self-identity.

In many religious traditions much emphasis is placed on the value of being Self-realized while, often, it is also taught that Self-realization is difficult to "attain." The very idea that this ideal state is to be attained or acquired is a delusion, an invalid belief. Self-realization is not a state or condition to earn or possess. It is a realization to which we awaken, to discover that, at our core, we have always been enlightened, knowledgeable, and free.

CHAPTER THREE

Meditation Techniques and Routines to Use for Satisfying Results

Meditation techniques are like tools we use to accomplish specific purposes. When we no longer need our tools we can put them away. Use meditation techniques to elicit the relaxation response and to facilitate adjustments of states of consciousness, then discard them and let meditation flow.

The purpose of using a meditation technique is to improve concentration and facilitate adjustments of states of consciousness. They are not magical processes; they involve our attention and regulate mental and physical states so that our awareness, removed from distracting influences, becomes clear. The key to effective use of a meditation technique is to give attention to it without trying to force results. We cannot successfully create clear states of consciousness; we can only be instrumental in removing obstacles to awakening and unfoldment.

The clear states of consciousness we aspire to experience are not caused by our endeavors. They naturally unfold when conditions are most suitable for them to do so. We should not attempt to induce moods which make us feel good and thus lull us into a complacent emotional state, or to use self-suggestion or controlled visualization processes to create imaginary mental states. Our meditation aim should be higher than merely an improved state of conditioned consciousness; we should aspire to have awareness removed from mental processes by awakening to superconscious states, which transcend them.

While it is helpful to be personally instructed in meditation procedures by someone who is proficient in practice, the basic techniques described here can be learned and used with benefit by carefully reading the explanations and experimenting with them. The recommended way to proceed is to use them routinely without expectation of dramatic results, patiently allowing sequential meditation practice sessions to afford you time and opportunity to learn. The following meditation techniques have been used for centuries because experience has proven their usefulness.

1. **Relaxation Technique:** Suitable for anyone, to elicit the relaxation response for the purpose of experiencing the restorative, enlivening effects of mental calm and physiological rest. Sit for at least 20 minutes, mentally listening to a chosen word or word-phrase. Choose an agreeable word, such as peace, light, love, joy—any word with which you feel comfortable and has inspirational value to you. Or a word-phrase, such as, "I am peace," "I am light," "I am love," "I am joy"—or any words agreeable to you. In the latter instance, do not use the word-phrase as a self-suggestion for the purpose of trying to condition the mind or induce an emotional state. Use it

only to focus your attention.

When using a single word, sitting upright and still, with eyes closed and attention flowing to the higher brain, mentally repeat the word a few times, slowly and gently. Then, recalling the "sound" of the mentally spoken word, "listen" to that sound repeating itself in your field of awareness. That is, instead of continuing to mentally speak the word, let the word resonate in your field of awareness. Just give yourself to the listening process. Do this until your attention is internalized and still. Then, ignore the word and rest in the stillness until you feel inclined to conclude your practice session.

A word-phrase is used the same way. With it, as a preliminary stage of practice, you can begin by listening to the words synchronized with your breathing rhythm. To do this, sitting relaxed and alert, let breathing flow naturally. When inhalation occurs, mentally listen to "I am." When exhalation occurs, mentally listen to the second part of the word-phase. Continue for a while until you are relaxed and attention is somewhat internalized, then disregard the body's breathing process and give your attention only to the word-phrase which repeats in your field of awareness. As practice progresses, eventually disregard the word-phrase and rest in the deep silence until you feel inclined to conclude your practice session.

2. **Devotional Meditation Technique**: Used as above, with more devotional intention. Use the

word "God" or the word-phase "Om God" as your mantra. (See schedule number four, below, for more information about *Om*.) Proceed as with the basic relaxation technique, while more obviously letting your ego-sense (the learned or acquired sense of independent selfhood) dissolve, being open to apprehending and experiencing an awareness of the Presence and Reality of God. When the mantra falls away, feel yourself to be merged in God.

Extensive inquiry reveals that many individuals, who practice the relaxation meditation technique primarily for psychological and physiological benefits, tend to discontinue their practice after some improvement is experienced or because of losing interest. Those who include meditation in their daily devotional, religious, or spiritual routine, tend to maintain a regular meditation schedule.

3. **Sanskrit Mantras:** These mantras have the added value of their unique sound-frequency potency which can beneficially influence the mind and nervous system. They are used as are the words or word-phrases described above. Although it is usually more helpful to learn Sanskrit mantras during an occasion of personal instruction—to be sure you know what the mantras sound like and how to use them— you can experiment with them to see if they serve your purposes.

Begin with *hong sau* (hong-saw). Let the first syllable float in your field of awareness when you breathe in; let the second syllable float in your field of awareness when you breathe out. Feel that the sounds are emerging from the boundless field of pure consciousness into your field of awareness. As your practice progresses, disregard the breathing process, listening to the mantra until awareness of it ceases or you go beyond it into the deep silence.

Or use *so ham* (so-hum) just as *hong sau* is used. With *so ham* you can, if you want to, also contemplate the meaning of the mantra as it flows: "Pure Consciousness–am I." When the mantra drops away, continue to contemplate pure, existence-being as your essential nature.

4. **Om Mantra Technique:** All mantras derive their potency from *Om* because from this primordial energy-force all things come into expression. "In the beginning was the Word, and the Word was with God, and the word was (is) God. All things were made by it, and without it was not anything made that was made." (New Testament, *Gospel of St. John*: 1:1 & 3). Also, Patanjali's *Yoga Sutras,* (1:27-29): "The manifesting symbol (evidential aspect) of God is *Om*. One should meditate on this Word, contemplating and surrendering to it. Meditation on *Om* results in cosmic consciousness and the removal of all mental and physical obstacles to success on the spiritual path."

This technique can be used after preliminary techniques have been used or it can be used alone. The easy way is to assume your meditation posture and begin with your usual preliminary procedure (settling down, prayer and/or invocation of God). Then proceed in five progressive stages. 1) Chant *Om* (*O-o-o-o-o-m-mn*). Let it flow out easily, concluding with a slight nasalization sound, a blending of *m* and *n*. Chant it quietly several times, medium-slow and steady. 2) Continue to chant, but more softly. 3) Chant in a whisper, going more within. 4) Mentally chant, going still more deeply within and listening in the inner ear canals to any subtle sound that might be discerned. 5) Cease mental chanting while continuing to "listen" to the mental sound resonating in your field of awareness. If you can actually hear a subtle, continuous sound in your ears or as though pervading your field of awareness, give your attention to that. Know *Om* to be all-pervading, emanating from the field of God's omnipresent consciousness, the substratum, the supporting essence, of everything in the field of creation. Feel yourself dissolving in *Om*. Expand your awareness in *Om*. Lose your sense of independent selfhood while being aware of your existence as *Om*. Know that the source of *Om* is the field of God. Contemplate the reality of God. Go beyond all ideas and concepts of God to the transcendental reality of God: to absolute, pure, existence-being. There, rest.

5. **Inner Light Technique:** Look within, with awareness focused in the spiritual eye and upper brain. Gaze beyond the spiritual eye, looking steadily into the distance of inner space. Feel that your awareness is not confined to the skull, that

you exist in boundless space. Do this when you are very calm, when breathing is slow and thoughts are minimal. Be aware, without effort, as an observer, and wait. If you perceive light at the spiritual eye or become aware of it in the higher brain, experience it. Merge in it, gently contemplate its origin—and what is behind it. You can contemplate inner light exclusively, or you can contemplate it along with practice of the *Om* technique. Light perception may be the result of stimulation of the optic nerves, so don't presume it to be a supernatural event. Just use the technique to focus attention and further internalize it. Eventually transcend light perception, to experience pure being.

Remember that meditation techniques are preparatory procedures: preliminary practices to use until spontaneous unfoldments of refined states of consciousness occur—as they can and will when inner restrictions to their flows are weakened or removed. Because our innate, soul urge is to have awareness restored to wholeness, this impulse will direct the meditation process when our preparation allows it to be influential. All obstacles to successful practice of meditation can be noted and overcome by patient practice. After the practice of a meditation technique, sit for a long time in the silence. Sometimes, just sitting in the silence with an alert, watchful attitude, is more effective than using a specific meditation technique. Use techniques to calm physical and mental processes and to internalize attention, then let meditation unfold without conscious effort on your part. Some disturbing factors are:

• *Environmental Disturbances* – Noise, excessive heat or cold, and other conditions which may interfere with meditation practice should be avoided.
• *Lack of Knowledge About the Process* – This obstacle to successful practice is easily overcome by acquiring knowledge and applying it correctly. Even right knowledge, if incorrectly applied, is not useful. Meditation techniques vary, but the inner way to soul awakening is the same for everyone. Don't be mislead by anyone who tries to tell you that their mantra or special technique is better than the ones you are learning here. All valid techniques serve the same purpose: that of improving powers of concentration and nurturing awakened spiritual consciousness.
• *Physical Discomfort* – Sit in an upright, comfortable posture. Have a comfortable chair for this purpose. If you prefer to sit on the floor with legs crossed, this is all right so long as you are comfortable. For prolonged meditations, you may want to place a small cushion or folded blanket between your lower back and the chair, to provide support. If physically unwell and unable to sit upright, then pray and experience the silence in a reclining position. Unless unable to do so, meditate in an upright, seated posture to ensure an alert attitude.
• *Emotional Distress* – With practice, train yourself to remove attention from circumstances which

may contribute to emotional distress. Learn to put such matters out of your mind when you go to your meditation chamber. Do not use your meditation practice time to engage in self-analysis. If you have problems that need to be solved, give your attention to doing so after deep meditation. If you are so emotionally distressed that you cannot meditate, disregard meditation until you are capable of practicing with clear intention. Pray for strength, and learn practical ways to solve your problems.

• *Subconscious Resistance to Change* – One of the primary obstacles to successful meditation practice is the same restriction that prevents one from being successful in any other useful endeavor—deep-seated, subconscious resistance to change of any kind. Being "more comfortable" with conditions as they are, even if they are not satisfying, or being afraid of change of any kind, may cause us to either deny that change is necessary or to defend our present condition. We may then go through the motions of trying to help ourselves while, at a deeper level, being unwilling to allow ourselves to experience emotional and spiritual growth. Disinterest, laziness, refusal to learn, procrastination, mental perversity, and all of the other self-defeating attitudes and behaviors common to the self-conscious condition, should be renounced. To replace these life-restricting attitudes and behaviors, cultivate lively curiosity, enthusiasm, enjoyment of learning and growing, willing attention to duty, receptivity to worthwhile ideas, and attitudes and behaviors which expand awareness and nurture wellness and actualization of soul capacities. The solution to resistance to change is to acquire a more complete philosophical understanding.

• *Preoccupation with Mental Transformations* – So long as we are identified with ever-flowing mental transformations, meditation practice will be restricted. The wavelike actions which occur in the mental field may be caused by our own endeavors to process information or by impulses arising from deeper levels of the unconscious. In the former instance, mental activities occur in response to our inclination to engage in rational thinking or to analyze memories. In the latter instance, even when we prefer to experience mental peace, physical or emotional discontent, the habit of being outwardly directed, or restlessness, may start the movement of subtle impulses which then cause persistent movements in the mental field.

When preoccupied with rational thinking, although useful insights can sometimes be intellectually determined, attention tends to remain involved at the level of mundane concerns.

When preoccupied with delusions (invalid beliefs or opinions), thinking is confined to self-centered themes, clouding reason and preventing the unfoldment of transformative insights.

When preoccupied with illusions (misperceptions of what is being observed or analyzed), thinking will be irrational and conclusions will be invalid or erroneous. Thus, even occasional intuitive insights and superconscious perceptions and experiences will be misunderstood, resulting in fantasy and, perhaps, hallucination. Meditators who are subject to illusional thinking may tend to desire phenomenal perceptions: to communicate with "angels" or "spirit guides," to have "revelations" which will provide meaning to their lives or allow them to feel themselves to be special or unique. Even sincere devotees on the spiritual path with minimal ego needs may tend to remain fixated in their illusions because of erroneously believing them to be genuine realizations.

When preoccupied with memories, meditative concentration for the purpose of experiencing refined superconscious states or to apprehend the nature of higher realities, is impossible to implement or to be maintained.

Preoccupation with normal cycles of mental transformations may influence the meditator to engage in twilight sleep—wakefulness mixed with subconscious perceptions—or to actually drift into a sleep state when meditating. To avoid doing this, one should meditate when rested and alert, maintain an upright meditation posture, keep attention flowing inward and upward, and remain attentive to the meditation technique being implemented while aspiring to transcendental perceptions and realizations. Sincere interest in spiritual growth possibilities, devotion to God (or to the ideal to be apprehended and experienced), and alert, dedicated practice will keep attention flowing to superconscious levels so that subconscious and unconscious states are avoided.

• *Other Egocentric Involvements* – When we are egocentric, we tend to focus upon whatever will support our narrow sense of self-importance. When this tendency is allowed to be influential during our practice of meditation, we may be inclined to indulge in endeavors to create illusory mental states, or pleasant moods or emotional states which provide a degree of superficial enjoyment. We may be overly fascinated with fleeting perceptions, or indulge ourselves in becoming attached to enjoyable sensations when energy flows are experienced or shifts of states of consciousness occur. While the effects of meditation practice can be enjoyable, clinging to them is a mistake. Whatever we perceive or experience that is, because of its inherent character, transitory, should be allowed to pass so that permanent, authentic experience of our real nature can be realized.

CHAPTER FOUR

Awakening Through Progressive Stages of Spiritual Growth

While on the spiritual growth path our inner journey is from our present level of understanding to full enlightenment—to complete knowledge and experience of ourselves as individualized units of Universal Consciousness. As spiritual growth progresses, constructive, life-enhancing improvements in our personal circumstances naturally unfold because inner states of consciousness always reflect as outer conditions. We perceive more clearly, our functional abilities are more result-producing, and we are healthier and more open to life. This is how we are able to know that our spiritual growth is genuine or authentic.

The awakening process is slow, steadily progressive, or rapid, depending upon the knowledgeable attention we give to it. Casual involvement produces minimal results. Well-intentioned but unfocused endeavors produce corresponding results. Total dedication to right practices produces superior results.

There are seven broad categories or stages of soul perception and experience. By knowing our present stage of unfoldment in relationship to higher levels which are attainable, and by knowing how to prepare ourselves for further awakening, we can facilitate progressive spiritual growth. If we know what we need to do to nurture desired changes—and do it—we can experience a quickening of our spiritual evolution and awaken to complete Self-knowledge which will result in freedom in space-time in the present sojourn on earth. We are free, or liberated, when delusions and illusions are entirely absent from our field of awareness.

The seven broad categories or levels of soul unfoldment are:

• *Relatively Unconscious* – In this condition one is self-conscious, with clouded awareness. Valid knowledge of one's spiritual nature and of higher realities is virtually nonexistent. One is strongly identified with body and mind, with an instinctual tendency to be primarily motivated to satisfy physical and emotional needs. Attachments to beliefs and traditional ways of doing things is usually evident. One may be a good or decent person but the mental attitude is usually provincial, or contractive. If interested in spiritual matters, one may be satisfied with a traditional religious affiliation and with a fixed belief system. If such people meditate correctly, with an open-minded attitude, spiritual growth will gradually occur.

• *Subconscious* – Self-conscious awareness with attitudes and behaviors primarily influenced by moods, whims, habits and desires, and thinking confused by illusions. Intellectual discernment is faulty. Fantasy is appealing. Emotional immaturity is common, as is self-delusion. Tendencies to addictive behaviors and relationships, and to self-defeating behaviors, may complicate one's life. If interested in spiritual matters, one may be enthralled with philosophical systems and religious practices which are new, different, exotic, or other-worldly and impractical. Restlessness and mental perversity (the tendency to interpret even valid information for self-serving purposes) may be apparent. Meditators at this level need to avoid preoccupation with egocentric needs, mental phenomena, and various transitory perceptions that unfold. They are advised to adhere to the purpose of meditation practice, which is to awaken to superconscious states. They need to cultivate a lifestyle which will establish them in behaviors and relationships which will keep them grounded and on a practical, purposeful course in life.

• *Self-conscious* – The state in which one has a clear sense of self-identity and self-determination. At this level one is usually intellectually discerning, skillfully functional, and able to provide for the necessities of life and to accomplish purposes without too much difficulty. If attention is mostly outward, one can be successful in the secular world. Egocentric drives may cause one to mistakenly assume that he or she is in complete control of destiny. Power, control, and acquiring material things, or status, may be prevailing drives. If one is interested in spiritual matters, the primary inclination may be to think in terms of "what's in it for me?" instead of "what is life for?" At this level one may be able to fairly easily understand physical, mental, and metaphysical principles of causation—how to accomplish purposes

or create circumstances—but may not be wisely
motivated. There is a difference between knowledge
and wisdom: knowledge is information; wisdom is
knowing how to use it. Meditation may be practiced
primarily for the life-enhancement benefits (which
are of value) while aspiration to higher realizations
may be modest. Meditators at this level need to also
think in terms of service. They should ask: How can
I use my talents and abilities in the most worthwhile
ways, for my highest good and the highest good of
others and the world?

• *Superconscious* – Degrees of soul awareness
which enable one to discern that "I-ness" is other
than mental or physical, that awareness includes
more than gross matter conditions. At this level one
is usually committed to the ideal of further awakening and rapid spiritual growth. Intellectual powers
are more dependable because fewer delusions and
illusions cloud mental processes. Intuitive abilities
are more pronounced. At this level, one may pray
for a relationship with a true guru (enlightened
spiritual teacher) or for the dissolving of any remaining ego-sense so that more expanded states of
consciousness can be experienced. One at this level
is an ideal disciple, learning quickly and effectively
practicing what is learned. During meditation practice, the primary aspiration is to experience subtle
and refined states of superconsciousness and to
awaken to higher realities.

• *Cosmic Conscious* – Because of superconscious influences acting upon the mind and physiology during

ordinary, everyday circumstances, the mental field is purified and the body is refined so that expanded states of consciousness are normal. Perception of the fact that one Being, Life, Power, and expressive Substance exists, provides awareness of oneness or wholeness. In preliminary stages one may experience a sense of double-consciousness—perceptions of relative phenomena along with perceptions and knowledge of transcendental realities. When one is stable in cosmic consciousness, realization of the omnipresence, omnipotence, and omniscience of Universal Consciousness persists. Meditation practice is spontaneous, with attention freely flowing to transcendental levels. Life is lived selflessly with the full support of nature's influences. Desires are effortlessly fulfilled. Needs are easily met. Limiting beliefs of every kind, including that of death or nonexistence are absent.

• *God-Conscious* – The reality of God is known as God *is*—as the only expressive Being, Life, Power, and Presence from which the worlds and souls emanate. As with early superconscious and cosmic conscious stages of spiritual unfoldment, awakening to this level is usually progressive. Insights dawn, and perceptions provide knowledge which is validated by experience. This stage is beyond even the most refined intellectual ability to know. It is, usually, first intuitively apprehended, then directly experienced or realized. One at this level may outwardly conform to any wholesome lifestyle while engaging in self-responsible actions without experiencing any veiling or clouding of realization. During early stages, when God-consciousness is not complete, one should maintain a regular routine of spiritual practices for the purpose of removing remaining delusions and illusions from the mental field. When God-consciousness is complete, the soul is liberated from former restrictions.

• *Enlightenment* – Flawless realization (with knowledge) of the allness of Consciousness: from the field of pure existence-being (that which is absolute, unmodified or pure), to God, Cosmic or Universal Mind, the primordial field of unmanifest nature, and the causal, astral, and matter realms. When established at this stage there is no other level to experience and nothing more to know. Fully enlightened souls live in the world only to fulfill evolutionary purposes and to assist souls to their higher good.

Awakening through the progressive stages of spiritual growth may be experienced during meditation. The stages we move through may also be recognized as we observe ourselves actualizing constructive psychological changes and demonstrating improvements in functional abilities. We may notice that our problem-solving abilities become more pronounced, insights enable us to know what we did not know before, and that our way of viewing life is increasingly more universal and decidedly more satisfying. While revealing meditation perceptions are satisfying at the subjective level, the life-enhancing changes we experience while engaged in objective relationships validates our spiritual progress and makes life more enjoyable.

When meditating, some discernible signs of superconscious awareness are mental peace, emotional calm, and a secure sense of being inwardly centered while being alert and attentive to what is occurring. We may still be aware of fluctuating moods and shifting mental processes but we are a witness to them and not as involved with them as we formerly were. At this stage the meditator may doubt the validity of the experience even though it is pleasant and the aftereffects are beneficial. With repeated practice of superconscious meditation, doubts vanish as more expanded states of consciousness unfold.

Every mental perception leaves an impression or memory. Mental impressions resulting from environmental stimulation and our own thoughts, moods, and desires, are not always constructive in their further influences. However, the impressions resulting from superconscious experiences are always entirely constructive, and tend to weaken and neutralize destructive mental impressions. This is why self-defeating habits and behaviors often fall away after one has been meditating on a regular schedule for a few weeks or months. Another reason why such habits and behaviors can be more easily renounced when a spiritual growth program has been implemented, is that, with new resolve, one is inspired to make better choices. When a sense of enlightened purpose is the determining factor, we are naturally inclined to direct our energies and resources to meaningful ends.

The mental impressions of superconscious perceptions are also eventually dissolved when full illumination of mind and consciousness is experienced. One is then no longer influenced by mental conditionings. Instead, intuitive guidance directed by innate intelligence determines actions.

The ideal approach to spiritual growth is to aspire to it with dedicated devotion, remaining inwardly centered and patient while growth occurs in time. Regardless of what your present degree of spiritual understanding might be, whether clouded or more clear, inwardly hold fast to the knowledge that you are a spiritual being endowed with all of the attributes and capacities common to every other soul in the universe. This is the absolute truth.

God is the only Being in existence. You are an individualized ray or unit of God's consciousness. This fact cannot be changed. Therefore, you are endowed with innate knowledge which has but to be awakened and actualized. Never say, or think, that you are anything less than what you are as an immortal, spiritual being. The habits, viewpoints, feelings, desires—and all else that might be presently influential that comprises your self-conscious condition—are temporary. They are superimposed upon your awareness but they are not the real *you*. They are not the final, determining circumstances of your life. They are impermanent, therefore, temporary, and you are superior to them. Everything that needs to be changed will be transformed as you awaken steadily through progressive stages of spiritual growth.

While on the awakening path, remember that the path is not the destination: it is only the way. Do not tarry when it is unnecessary. Look forward to the ultimate outcome, to what will be true for you when your awakening is complete. Remember, too, that though spiritual growth is usually progressive, there is always the possibility of sudden awakening— unanticipated breakthroughs, occasions when clear perception and knowledge blossoms and vast regions of mind and consciousness are revealed. Your dedicated practices and adherence to right living routines are but preparation. When the moment is right, when you are prepared and are responsive to grace, its redemptive actions will remove the cloud of unknowing from your mind and the light of understanding will brilliantly shine.

Grace is the enlivening life (spirit) of God supporting and transforming creation. It expresses throughout the field of nature and from within every soul. It directs the course of evolution and awakens souls from their "sleep" of mortality. When we are less self-centered and more soul-centered, less grasping and more giving, less contractive and more expansive, grace more obviously expresses to order our lives and our circumstances.

CHAPTER FIVE

Lifestyle Guidelines Supportive of Our Primary Aims and Purposes

Although it is true that regular, right practice of meditation does beneficially influence our lives and contribute to useful changes and helpful improvements, we can assist ourselves to complete wellness and more skillful function by intentionally implementing constructive lifestyle routines. The guiding principle for doing this is that everything we do should fully support our primary purposes for which we are in this world. We have four primary purposes to fulfill. They are easy to remember and essential to actualize:

• *To Live Right* – We are living in the right way when we are self-responsible, successfully fulfilling our duties and obligations, and using our talents and abilities to make useful contributions to society and the planet. We know we are "in our right place in life" when we are soul-content and so in accord with circumstances that all aspects of our lives are balanced and harmonious.

• *To Learn to Have Our Life-Enhancing Desires Easily Fulfilled* – By learning how to use our intelligence and abilities to live successfully, and by learning how to adjust our mental attitude and states of consciousness, we can experience easy fulfillment of life-enhancing desires. Desires which, if fulfilled

would interfere with the unfoldment of higher purposes, should be renounced. Become proficient in
endeavors. Learn how to cooperate with mental and
metaphysical principles of causation. Live without
strain. Be a gracious, cultured, knowledgeable, successful person.

• *To be Affluent* – If we resist the idea of being
affluent ("in the flow of life"), we restrict life's inclination to thrive, to flourish, to be successful in the
accomplishment of its purposes. The universe is
self-complete, whole. When we are in harmony with
its actions we are included in its processes and all
of our needs are spontaneously met. When we are
affluent, we can almost effortlessly fulfill all of our
endeavors.

• *To be Spiritually Enlightened* – If we are successful in learning how to function as social beings but
have not yet experienced authentic spiritual growth,
our lives are not complete. Therefore, include spiritual studies and practices in your daily routine, and
do your best to live from your highest level of understanding. You will grow to emotional maturity and
awaken to flawless knowledge of your real nature
and your relationship with the Infinite.

Come to terms with the fact that you are in relationship with life for a purpose. Find out what that
purpose is and fulfill it. You will then fulfill your
spiritual destiny. Merely to be inclined to drift with
the tides of circumstances, or to focus on satisfying
petty personal desires and whims, is to waste the

precious opportunity living in this world provides. There is no better place than where we are to learn our lessons and to awaken and express our spiritual capacities. Have you wasted time, energy, and resources in the past because of purposeless or misguided endeavors? If so, release the past and resolve to do better from now on. Are you wasting time, energy, and resources now? If so, choose to think, feel, and behave more constructively.

Regardless of present circumstances, be they oppressive, or more supportive but not fulfilling, all that is needed to implement useful change in the direction of more freely expressive life is choice. When we choose more ideal circumstances, we make decisions. When we make decisions, our thought processes become more organized and rational. We enter into a cooperative relationship with the enlivening Power that nurtures the universe—and us—and, being responsive to It, discover that we are supported by currents of life which carry us along and provide for our well-being through every stage of our awakening, learning, and growing.

Right knowing, right relationship with the Infinite, and right living, is the way to confirm our dedication on the awakening path and to prove to ourselves the authenticity of our spiritual growth.

—INTENTIONAL PRACTICE GUIDE—

Our understanding determines the usefulness of our choices, and living with intention facilitates emotional, intellectual, and spiritual growth. Do these things with conscious intention:

What is the highest good you can see for yourself?

_____

What will you do to actualize it or experience it?

_____

_____

_____

_____

Read this book several times, marking the ideas and themes that speak to you. On another sheet of paper, or in your personal journal, write your plans and projects for living with worthwhile purpose. Write your spiritual practice routine.

SPEAK THIS AFFIRMATION
I open my mind and being to my endless good.
I acknowledge the truth—that I am a spiritual
being forever established in wholeness. I will
live wisely, act with conscious intention, and live
always in tune with the Infinite.

Center for Spiritual Awareness is an enlightenment movement with offices and retreat center in the mountains of northeast Georgia. Meditation retreats are offered from early spring through late autumn. An active publishing program includes the production and international distribution of books, monthly lessons, the bimonthly *Truth Journal* magazine, and audio tapes. Affiliated meditation groups are active in many cities of the United States and in other countries. Roy Eugene Davis is the spiritual director.

For a free literature packet describing our publications and varied services, use the address or telephone numbers provided below:

Center for Spiritual Awareness
Post Office Box 7
Lakemont, Georgia 30552-0001
U.S.A.

(706) 782-4723 Weekdays   Fax (706) 782-4560

Note: You are cordially invited to share copies of *An Easy Guide to Meditation* with people you know to be sincerely interested in spiritual growth. You may order from the address above. For 1 copy $2.00 plus $1.00 for postage and handling.

Two or more copies $1.00 each, shipping free.

Booksellers may order at usual trade discounts.